INSIDEOUTSIDE

Also by New Academia Publishing

NO BARKING IN THE HALLWAYS: Poems for the Classroom, by Ann Bracken
AT THE END OF THE SELF-HELP ROPE: Poems, by Ed Zahniser
MASS FOR NANKING'S 1937, by Wing-chi Chan
THE HOUR OF THE POEM POEM: Poems on Writing, by David Bristol
THE WHITE SPIDER IN MY HAND: Poems, by Sonja James
THE ALTAR OF INNOCENCE: Poems, by Ann Bracken
THE MAN WHO GOT AWAY: Poems, by Grace Cavalieri
IN BLACK BEAR COUNTRY, by Maureen Waters
ALWAYS THE TRAINS: Poems, by Judy Neri

Read an excerpt at www.newacademia.com

INSIDEOUTSIDE

Poems by
Sue Silver

WASHINGTON, DC

Library of Congress Control Number: 2017933800
ISBN: 978-0-9986433-0-4, paperback (alk. paper)

 An imprint of new Academia Publishing

 New Academia Publishing
4401-A Connecticut Avenue NW #236
Washington DC 20008
info@newacademia.com
www.newacademia.com

To my children Pip, Hillary and Grayson

ACKNOWLEDGEMENTS

"What Would You Do," "In The Mercy of Stillness," "Heavy Rains,"
   "Dark Water," and "Night Listening" were published on the Dan
   Murano Arts and Letters website; "Heading That Way" in *Lummox
   Press #3*; and "Dreaming a Few Lines of Poetry" in the *Anthology of
   Appalachian Writers* Vol. IV.
"The Lamp" appeared in *Amepoesis* and "The Doctor Said" in
   Poets&Artists.

THANKS: To my Spiritual Teacher Sai Maa and my fabulous poetry
   mentor Grace Cavalieri.
   Thank you, Maa, for your love and your grace for helping me
      uncover my heart.
   Thank you, Grace, for believing in me and helping me uncover
      my voice.
   To all those who have helped me in my life, thank you.

CONTENTS

A BIT OF WEATHER

The clouds roiled
through the windows we watched
as the boats bucked at their moorings
and the wind wept.
Now sailing in the
clouds, tall as skyscrapers
pinching the light
measuring night in
mustering the vast seas
moving with the moon
our tyrant of the sky.

WHAT WOULD YOU DO?

A Poem After Mary Oliver

What if a hundred eagles
called you by your name and flew above you.
What if a crow sat at your window
told you how to fix your printer.
What if the summer breeze
took away your aches and pains.
What if the whistle from the passing train
gave you an idea
and you became filled with joy.
What if the news was filled with
stories of goodness in the world
and all hostilities ceased.
What if the light in our eyes became so bright
we couldn't kill each other any more.
What if you finally knew the value of your every breath
the way the flower turns its face to the sun.

BEFORE THE STORM

The birds are dancing themselves down to perch,
turning and swooping

dropping down to rise, then up, breaking off
from each other to a smaller group,

just enough to make it comfortable for landing.
They seek shelter before a night rain

that marches its band across the western horizon
with the lightest of breezes.

As the birds move through the sky, I see the full black wing silhouette
turn to the barest sliver

then become mere dots flashing downward,
then upward, spiraling a circular swirl

then, hanging in air as a landing group
wheels down and down.

They make a distinct *thwap* to my limbs,
my body swaying with their bird movements,

my heart alive with little bird hearts.
Not many of my leaves have fallen

and many are still green.
They land with one voice, then quiet

as more of this great flock fills my branches.
I see their airy motions as they move

'till all have landed. Quiet settles,
just before the rains, the nestling in of bodies

to my bark, my skin, a place of comfort. Their hearts
a rapid swelling of life to my slow breaths.

AT THE AIRPORT

Waiting at the airport, hour after hour
the lengthy madness
floating in the airport aura I am present to,
laughing workers moving by
their bond, the longed for forgotten in this daily event
waiting, writing, big planes coast by
en route to runways, distant gates.

Sun on a hazy tarmac, where a boarding stairway stands alone
food and luggage carts driven by at a good clip
voices waft, phone conversations
overhead announcements, the jagged security warnings, again and
        again,
hot tea at the café, a somewhat dry sandwich,
the wait goes on, ah but here, a stillness arises.

INSIDE OUTSIDE

I am from infant failing to thrive
infant restored with intramedullary feedings,
saved with Mother's milk.
I am from always the new person on the block.
Milk bottles delivered to the house
air raid drills under the desk,
Rock 'n Roll and Elvis.

I am from the ocean, clean salty swell, surfing the waves
on 8 foot boards at Piha beach, black sands and riptides,
sweet parties at the Surf Club, 1960's,
scuba diving in the caves of the Poor Knights Islands.
I have travelled on the "Oronsay" to this new home down under
the land of the Long White Cloud, New Zealand,
the Maori, mother's friends and family.

I am from divorce and decree, Catholic school and rules,
writing, writing and my first Brownie camera.
Poetry, stories and photographs.
The Newmarket Swim club, sunburn and swim meet.
I am from the red phone box, press button B to speak.
The sailboat adventures, aboard the 36 foot sloop of friends—
winning the race at the Akarana Yacht Club and
night time sailing in the cold, warmed with coffee and a drop of rum.

Nursing school and Postgraduate studies, the Ann Arbor riots.
I am from Meditation, Kriya Yoga, energy healing and growth,
Soul retrieval,
Transformation, my Beloved Guru, Sai Maa,
travelling always through profound healings.

DARK WATER

The dark waters, brown colored
in their depths, know nothing of my blood
running out from this deep gash
while fishing, this new knife unwieldy in my hands.

The kindness of strangers
asking if I'd caught anything
helping in my distress to bind my wound
stem the flow for all I know
the uncaught fish sallying for light
caught in a flash of reflection
watched me from beneath the pier
amazed at my ignorance, eating gladly
the bloodworm I dropped there.

At the hospital the nurses take such care
I am swept and cleaned and stitched
the lost light of this lovely afternoon
a picture past.

I visit again this windy pier
I do not cast nor attend to fishing gear
but walk and sit and linger in the cold
and ask the fish for another year.

SWEETNESS

Here I am with sweetness.
Sweetness, a pause from the painful...
The broken heart
bruised lip, ringing ears.

In the dim light
your hand and still there's this,

That which dwells in the center of our hearts,
on the lips of the Beloved. The kiss of the Divine
comes to me in her many forms, so beautiful, so varied. The breath of the
breeze, the sweep of the storming winds.

In the mercy of stillness
regret cannot enter
nor journey to its center.
It has no mode of transport there.
The quick Light dives deep.
That is the way of sweetness.

DO YOU KNOW OF TREES?

Do you know how trees breathe us?
Their deep life
What do we know?

Look here
the snow studded limbs iced over, glistening,
moving silently through the window
piney branches delicately waving to wind's quick breath.

Do we know how they are with other trees?
Perhaps speaking with the breath of wind,
speaking through soil, earth entwined roots,
weaving down and through and deep.

These trees have a magnificence in their ways.
As I walk through woods, perfumes of
opening buds in May.
Each a planet of life, for birds and bugs.

In summer passing through walls of green
a spell of beauty
whole trees blossoming
painted bright with life.

TIME TRAVEL

Time has somehow slipped away
lies hidden in the folds of the couch
frayed ends of covers and the bed.
Moments in the garden where the weeds crouch low,
but not so that the tulip cannot grow—

I lost an hour and a day
just cleaning up the cobwebs and the dust.
Pale moments meditating in my chair
so Light Divine could find me there
and writing this tears rush my heart
so filled with love for you,
my dearest patient, friend.

My Beloved holds my hand expands the wave.
I do not spend a moment where
this breath alone—that breathes me here,
no, time may slip or lie quite still
and claim a place for all I AM
for I AM all, I never knew the thought,
but know the place beginning and without end.

OUT FISHING

In early September some trees leaves
dry out quick giving up their chlorophyll early,
the green of their goodness,
oxygen capturing substance.
They float downstream with the bulging river
high from upstream rain.

My fishing buddy Rooster rolls
over the rocks on the riverbed
where we wade, gives me some
hellgrammites for bait.

I catch three bluegill with one and further upstream
three more and a smallmouth bass with a crawdad.

The sky is somewhat overcast
cooler air and the river like glass.
The white bones of the sycamore reflected.
And upstream past the big bend the Eagle
solemnly wings back to his high perch.

Sun breaks through, casts an eye.
I cast top water with my new Hula Popper.

With the sweetness of the air the crickets whirr
as we wade, a trill cheep
of hummingbird overhead
Water lights rippling on white boughs
catch my eye

13

a rolling line up the long bough
of the sycamore.

We pile back into the boat,
trees and river banks flash by with the pull of the motor.

Greens and yellows, trees reflected and two herons stalk the banks
one on each side of the river
while I, caught in the heart space of content,
fill my eyes.

WITHIN THE CIRCLES

How childlike of the trees
to cry their leaves down to the ground
then laugh and bare their naked limbs
to such a sky as might be passing by.

A cloud or two or numb,
bare naked in the temptress wind
and blackened with the dimming light
a child's sweet laugh, a movement

against the rising moon,
so within the circles of her years
she lives a mystery cell to cell both in and out
like my human bones a song of many lives

genetic wisdom
perhaps ignorance too in the passing of this
and the lack thereof that flexes a noose
of simple lines, not loosened yet by night

but freed in the breath
and ever new.

DREAMING A FEW LINES OF POETRY

In my dream a suited orator speaks a poem
A line I hear just before
waking. What was it now—
"the mother rain upon the earth?"

With exquisite diction, the antique fellow,
his honeyed voice and I impressed with the words.
What was it he said—
"and there the mother rain upon the earth?"

An apt beginning and on I write.
A washing rain soft at first
then a wall sluicing from the sky.
Lashing branches down

sweeping leaves and lines away
the rain watcher well back beneath the deep porch eave
as water washes pell mell and
gusting winds cross the lawn

and all before a feast, a tryst of weather
in the deep afternoon,
with darkness early upon me.
So suddenly stopping and still

just the drip from leaves to eaves
and the return of the hummingbird
to its evening meal. Ah yes…
"there the mother rain upon the earth."

FIREFLIES RISING

We sit together on the screened in porch
watch as the fireflies rise
light the grass tips with their glow
the sun long set behind the stand of trees
their leaves just burnt orange
a deep blue sky—
now stars and sweetness as the fireflies rise
from grass to hip-high—waving up the trees
rising with the night come down
to see these bright sparks,
small lives
and now to tree branches
spreading out
the fireflies take the night
rising, rising with their might.
Like the glow of love they go
and sweep a world aright.

DOG AND POET WALK

My dog Dingo and I will go
walking on the canal today
he'll be good with the gentle leader
and we'll listen to the birds.

One time I took him off his lead,
he raced up the hill after a bird
who whistled just like my son, Grayson.
came back all perplexed.

We'll listen to the wind
watch the river which will be up
with these rains—way up—
We won't get too close.

I'll take my pen and journal.
Perhaps a poem will come by,
floating on the waters
just in time.

NIGHT FISHING

The fishing boat departs at 6 pm, ticket in one hand
camera in the other, I board
and oh the knock your eyes out cloud action
is just beginning. Photography takes the fore
'till the other guys ask, "You here to fish or take pictures?"
But the skies are a riot of storm clouds.
We pause in our departure to let the
storm rush inland.

I am joined by two men, the Father-
in-law and son with their own rods
and gear, *mind if we sit here?*
At the inside table and bench and
the rolling boat as we speed out of the bay.
I am at the camera full on, on deck
starboard and port,
the cloud and sun reflections dancing through.
The men ready their gear, pull out
small fish for bait.

A young man comes by collecting for
the largest snapper pool.
$5 bucks, Sue, you can catch that, Sue!
Ya know you can. He's Dan
a real regular.
My girlfriend knows I'm fishing
Tuesdays and Thursdays no question!

It's all about the ride, rocking and rolling on the boat
tasty ocean breeze, seas a gunmetal blue.
The sea turtle off the boat bow
surfacing for a look, maybe some chum.

Young men help with the lines
setting bait
helping with a catch
gloved hands deft with the hook
and there are some beauties, big fish,
flopping and flailing.

I fish off the bow next to the well-geared guys
but I look bad, no catch, no bite.
I move to the starboard side
it's not easy with the boat rolling and I, a river
fisher, not used to this!

Cap'n moves the boat for better fishing
the anchor won't stay, drags off an edge.
"Pull up your lines, we're moving."
I can't catch a thing!
At the end of the trip two young ladies
give me their catch
15 snapper cleaned and filleted.

At home the crowd cheers. We fry them in olive oil and
a little pepper,
Delicious.

THE TEACHING

Who else holds this in memory?
In memory perhaps nothing the next day
until finally it is revealed.
A justness—would that there was justice in this world,
yet there she stands tattered.
Bent knuckles burned, scratched
and blistered.

I take it for granted
this strength of mind,
snapping back into place
after a bad run over something.

Fact is, I lose it just like the next guy
hold delusions some I don't even know I have.
You are strong or stronger, or the strongest
Wing nut holding engine together.
It's because I am smitten with love
for you and you and you.

An owl call wakes me in this tent
listening through
sounds of wind
snake me to sleep
down the long train of letting go to dreaming
a teaching waiting to be taken in.

NIGHT LISTENING

I listen to the crickets' droning whir
as if to pluck my dreams out of the sky,
nestled on my pillow it's a blur
I have to lift my head to listen more.

Listening with my whole self in the night
with dreams a lost repeated whirl
of incompletes and waking at the spool
unraveled thread, mostly awake
endures enduring all the night.

And still the crickets stitch the night
saying with their rhythmic song
secrets of the journey here
the mystery of night song born.

FIRE MOON

I love that huge harvest moon.
She rises slow in a deep blue sky
so close you could touch her,
that round full face golden against the darkening blue.

At Summer's close she hangs in the morning air
drifting out of sight into the long pale day
pulling herself away, a long slow kiss.

The long sounds of Summer nights
dancing weaving of dreams.
Life builds a future in the fruiting of the plantings.

Too soon comes Autumn blazing,
the harvest moon trumpet of the fall
the shout to replenish the stores.
Harvester of our journeys she rises, the fire moon.

CUTTING FIELDS

I see the big machines move methodically
across the soybeans
whose golden round fullness stretches
to the blade.

Over there, apple trees, felled to make way for new plantings.
I drive past tall brown stands of cornfields dried
within an inch of their lives.

The tractor moves across the now bare, red earth
the plains bending to the plane.

How sweet to be culled of our errant self
the demanding voice
the petulance of wanting constant and insidious.

Oh to let go to the sweetness of the inner stillness
the constancy of something greater.

Ah that which shines
the life force ...   Simple ever new.

HEAVY RAINS

It is raining a heavy cold rain
late August of this wet summer,
temperatures swinging to the lows.
An unusual summer
completely out of the ordinary,
like the large Grackle, that found
itself in the house today.

Not one of the three of us saw him enter
and he, frantic at the kitchen window,
looking for an immediate way out.

Not at first eyeing the open door
escape available
and then he took it, winging out,
his great silhouette against the Eastern sky.

This evening with the heavy rains,
an air, a promise of wood smoke
cozy nights by the fire,
hot soups and stews, their fragrances
lingering through the evening hours.

The evening hours when we will turn
our eyes to the winter moon and
wear the crisp starlit skies on our brow,
stamped and claimed with the
rhythms of our lives.

Like our peoples of ancient times
seeking miracles from an unknown world,
and making miracles in a new world.

MIRROR

In Africa whole cities blaze poverty.
No plumbing,
disease rampant.
On the plantations, servants work for pennies,
return to huts of paper and tin, no security.
Women raped at will.

There are the lies, boxed and marketed in attractive colors.
Like cigarettes, poison laced tobacco
corporate greed, addiction without knowledge,
going cheap
and over there to the market
rows of brightly colored fruits
99 cents to the seller, 1 cent to the grower.

In Nigeria bloody minded preachers stand
hawking witchcraft, blaming all the bad that goes down
on children calling them witches.
These innocent ones sent away abandoned
by their families, some as young as three.

Is this it then? Who will bring justice?
I look deeper in my own heart
thread the needle
of my own life.
How just am I?
Sand through my fingers
these thought waves
breaking shores
of my own making.
I must look deeper, deeper in my own heart
for the justice I hold.

HEADING THAT WAY

They say if you wish to reach enlightenment
you must lose your desires.

Well that's a tough one.
Why would I wish to give up my little wants

my wishes and the stuff that gets me outta bed
like earning that paycheck

so I can head home to New Zealand for eight weeks
whose lovely green shores, land of the long white cloud

I haven't set foot on for over 10 years.
See the faces, share the love with my family there,

I had to weep and when my old love met me
at the airport, his voice, his walk just the same in that corner

of my heart where we never let go.
How about that desire to scratch that itch?

Never mind the racks of clothes and shoes
the jewelry in that big glass case

I just want to hear the loudest thunder cracking overhead
waking me in my bed, sit on my porch and breathe the rain.

Just one more time, this time, I want to feel my heart
explode with love, know the joy, the tenderness in this moment.

RECIPE

Trying to order lunch is difficult
Soup salad or two soups…a quandary
Bread just makes me sleepy
Pizza days I'm all done in
Two slices one cookie I am
Asleep at the wheel
A pure postprandial coma.
Falling off the chair.
Now a hot lunch can be a treat
Hot turkey and veggies, rotisseries chicken
With mashed potatoes and greens.
The potatoes here are out of the box
I have developed a taste for them…mashed.

At home I cook soups
Thousand Dollar Chicken
Jane's recipe, who used to live with my friend Tom.
She hit him upside the head with a bag of change one time
Called the cops he went to jail…not her.
Cost him a thousand dollars.
It's really good chicken.

THE DAY TAKES OFF LIKE A ROCKET

The clock has no mercy for me
the day takes off like a rocket.

Birdsong fills the air as
trees bow their hurrah.

Gliding airwaves shake branches
and leaves
ride air tides so wildly sweet.

Walls of green, as I drive up this
mountain; birds are patterns in the sky
clouds move so fast quick shapes
unraveling by.

Once, my love, Lenny and I lived next door
to some kind of suspicious people.
Those neighbors came by sat around our
kitchen table, there in Redfern, Sydney.

They had come before and that woman
stared at me. She was rigid and reeked of meanness
wanting, wanting everything.

This time that guy she was with was all how are ya's
all smiles and how are ya's.
Maybe they wanted to see what we could see
out our window there that looked down on their place.

I walked around the kitchen
with my bag over my shoulder
the one with the picture of my
enlightened Master on it—before I left
for a stay with my sister.

Lenny told me later that after I left
they beat up everyone in the house,
dragged Pete from his bed.
took our cash and jewelry and trashed our house!

"And where were the dogs? I asked,
"our two big dogs, Fang and Wolf!
They would have been protecting us."
They gave them steaks out back,
I found the bones. They had tied the dogs up.

I thought of this as I drove, clouds racing above,
in another country, another time,
years later.
The house in Redfern, Sydney, Australia
and my life there.

AT THE FARM

In the big black 1946 Cadillac
To pick up Uncle from the plane

I said to Auntie, "tell him the black cat is waiting"
And she in delight replied,

Oh you tell him please do!
And it later became a family saying.

Now I frame photos of elderly aunts and us two kids,
With Mum on the front porch.

I take my brother to see the old place
He visits from NZ. We look again gazing

At the 200-year-old gracious brick farmhouse.
The lips of the creek holding the words of this family's history.

I wonder does she remember us
Swinging out tied in the arms of the weeping willow

Sitting in her waters gazing at the colors of her bones
The talking stones.

Once out where she dances in the pasture
My brother put the kittens in the water

To see if they could swim as I watched
Kneeling on the one plank bridge—

They were good swimmers
But I grabbed them out soaked and squealing

Wrapped them in my shirt.
At evening we chased fireflies

Catching them in jars
With bits of grass

To look at them up close
While the adults sipped mint juleps in sterling silver cups

With the mint we picked by the creek.
A stone cottage set a bit away from the house

A mystery of musky smells.
I found a dollhouse in it

With two floors and real windows
And a lock closure for the back

With carpets painted on the floors, tiny furniture and doors.
We rode in Auntie's car to Shepherdstown 1952

Sitting in the small jump seat
Frank Sinatra on my lips

A Mercedes Benz Sl 190.

IN SYNCH

Just as the cat food tin
rolls across the floor
lucky the lid is on tight,
as the bird alights on the branch, free of the stalking cat
in brief moments, life spills across the world
as present as the stillness after heavy snow,
the sudden crack of the branch breaking in the forest
the breath of a tree, the mist before a warming sun.
At dawn rising from her bed
sitting in meditation
allowing the silence to rise from her heart,
until her being spills over into the world.
The woman takes her world in her hands
measured breath to breath.
The life of the earth moving her forward.

CHISELING MY FATHER

Who could judge the chiseling skill
of pain.
Who sees it sneaking up?
The smashed milk jug,
a child's face bashed for the showing
a kitten the milk, and kicked aside.
"Oh brutal man
who made your life a war?"

THE TRADEOFF

"Stop it or I'll give you something to cry about!"
Dad shouts. I sob stifling them deep into myself.
cramming the sounds into my throat,
into my chest,

stuffing the tears down, compressing the pain
into my small, seven-year-old body.

Somehow I could stop, shuddering up the sobs
the uncontrollable tears wedged viselike in my hands
those clenched little mitts.

Dad saved my life when at six
I stuck my head out the window as Mom was driving into the garage
shouting at her to stop
and just in time I pulled my head into the car
merely a breath from decapitation.

THE ARRIVAL

We sit at the dining room table
the math books, all my homework
spread over the mahogany sheen.
How many hours
exhaustion takes my eyes
and still you push, expect,
demand.

In the car you drive me to school
The school Auntie pays for
50 miles away in Grosse Pointe at week's beginning
at week's end you pick me up,

and we must have talked, but I don't
remember what we said,
instead, I see you in your suit, your black felt hat
your long winter coat, smelling of Old Spice,
running up the stairs late,
so very, very late for the father-daughter dinner.

THE LAMP

They left us with warnings
as they went for the cocktail party—they had to go.
New in town,
"They'd be right back."
We were ages four and six
"Be good now, be good."

Brother starts the chase
suddenly the crash
the terror—the lamp
we try to fit the pieces together
small hands, big pieces
bent metal.

We hear the car tires on the cement
the lights reflected in the window
deadly silent in the room
the door opens and we are still by the lamp.
Then the shouting, then the screaming
then the shouting and the screaming
Down the dark wooden stairs to the basement
the strap is out, the belt

I watch my brother dancing to the sting
I know I will be next
now I am bent over the play chest
my legs are on fire and I throw up
all over the play chest

My mother on the stairs
"Oh Charles, Oh Charles"
We were only four and six.

CLOCK THROUGH THE WINDOW

Darkness is creeping in
we are moving quietly as we can

onto our neighbor's front porch to peer in the window
at that owl clock shining in the darkness

chiming and blinking through her window.
We are a bit late getting home

no chance now, the rush, the grab, the smack
should have been home 30 minutes ago

My father shouting *what do you think you're doing?*

the violent voice.

HIGHER

Mother accused me of being high on drugs
when I was me being high on life
higher than a kite soaring off to the edge of the moon,
"outta sight," as we said then.
Like crystals in the sand, sun cast and bending light rays
sweetness of nectar in the deep meditation moments
as it rises in your mouth sweet nectar.

Yes, Momma accused me of being too happy.
Too much I said to her sad self
detonated at that later date, by her suicide
when I was much too far away.

LAST TIME

The last time I saw my mother
in New Zealand so long ago
we visited, me with my two small children
and she fed my son so well, lamb chops on the bone
he gnawed at them with his two-year-old teeth and ate and ate.
And Hillary at four, Mum got her things to do
she really liked—

I couldn't tell my mother
the truth
how my life was falling apart
my husband leaving me
instead I found another face
a mask of lies
pretending to be whole—

How can we live so far apart
and now to come and be so lost—
my life so different at home in my other country
with work and work and so much responsibility.

The last time I saw my mother
I never really said good-bye
I was more afraid of her criticism—
than my need for love.

A POST CARDIAC SURGERY WARD

I wasn't at her bedside when death came
those eyes so large, open, staring
seeing nothing.
A child on the post cardiac surgery ward.
I was the lone night nurse on duty,
a second year student,
finding her like that on my rounds.

How did it come?
Was it a sudden, crushing pain, to her chest
a slowing of her heart rate, an embolus swift and still?
Was she asleep when death came?
Did someone miss a sign earlier?
These are the questions.

My heart aches for her aloneness.
No one at her bedside
holding her hand
and still, she had, I like to think a clean death.
I pray for her soul that she is happy.

But then I look at other children,
how they handle illness, some smiles, such strength.
I see the Divine so present in them.
I like to think it was this way with her.
A sweet 6-year-old, hand held by her angel,
walking into the Light.

THE MOTHER ON WARD THREE

I remembered her the other day
tears at that memory,
forgive me, forgive me.
I had visited her in the hospital even on my days off when
she had been transferred from my care to another unit.

They tell us in Nursing school, don't get attached to your patients.
A widow with three children aged 8, 10 and 12.
They would come to visit her in the hospital.
Sitting on her bed her dark hair veiling her cheek
as she touched an arm, held a hand.
A lung tumor.
The diagnoses came, she told me herself,
Cancer, she said flatly.

Not good in those days, the mid sixties.
Few treatments were successful.

I was overwhelmed ... the children
The children,

I didn't see her again.

REALIZATION

Today in one of the procedure rooms
a patient had a cardiac arrest.
Fear plucked my own heart
and ran up the meter.

This work is so damned hairy
human beings in our hands
the luff and lay of it all,
taking constant vigilance.

"How fragile we are."

Tonight after work
I did aerial yoga.
The beauty of it, wrapped in the long colorful silks
gliding into the shoulder stand resting there completely supported.

Now I meditate, enjoy the stillness within.
What great moments call us
this life blessed—
each breath a gift.

THE BIG MAN

This guy today must have been 325 lbs.
his jowls reached from his ears to his shoulders
and he was angry that he had to be there.
He was holding it in
angry at every movement of the bed
angry.

The Anesthesiologist said he was going to be
in the Procedure room with me,
the Nurse Anesthetist.
This was a two-person job.

Perhaps that anger is why this person eats and eats
to push it down
to be done, but he is never done
anger boils in his blood

his red face,
he was more than civil
but he was afraid just starting his IV,
terrible, a small child is better.

His case went well, he breathed well with the Doc's assistance
holding those massive jowls,
mask oxygen and the GI endoscope slipped through the hole
we made in the bottom right corner of the mask. The jaw thrust,
all helped and the sedation, just the right amount, so the patient
was comfortable and breathing well, amazingly, and we were pleased.

When it was over the patient thanked me again and again
he had come out of his fear
he had come out alive.

All I could think of was
what his wife said to me,
"Don't let anything happen to him
I put too much damned time and energy into him!"

I saw them leave,
her face like granite,
his very red and twitching.

THE DOCTOR SAID

A tall big boned woman, an Orthopedic Surgeon
where I was working as a nurse anesthetist
had been carrying this flag as long as I had known her.

"Oh, for Christ Sake!" she said,
"you have to at least check
for semen."

But why? She fell off the porch,
the ER Doctor said.

"Yeah, yeah she fell onto a stick
which just happened to jam into her
9-year-old vagina.
Please Jack, humor me.
All of us here all the Practitioners of this area
need to be aware and watch for sexual abuse.
Make the test, Jack."

In this small rural town there was so much that was
taken for granted, walked over, someone's cousin, a friend,
family.
        Everyone knew them, nothing wrong there,

and this was her fight,
her awareness.
Sexual abuse happening here, date rape, child abuse.
No time to pretend.

THE RIDE

I am hand ventilating a Preemie all four lbs. of her
my first ambulance transfer.
It is daylight around 11 am the roads are busy.
We weave and the driver presses into it.
An argument ensues about the speed of our vehicle.

I am concentrating on this tiny form, lifting the chest fast enough
giving the right amount of air,
watching her color. She is lying on a blanket on a tiny mattress.
I am sitting on a chair in the ambulance, she is my world.

It is just me, the baby and an ambulance tech.
The driver.
I saw him after it was all over,
he was sweaty and pale, a big man. He said,
When that woman started to pull out in front of us from the grocery store
I thought we were all going to die.

THE GIRLS

On the Pediatric ward,
two young girls with leukemia
Their parents—stunned—agonized
with all the decisions
and we the nurses looking on
waiting and watching for their decision.

One set of parents were aghast overcome at such a level
they couldn't speak for days.
They sat, gazing at their child, holding her hand, stroking her brow
with such love and yearning. We did our work tenderly and
carefully as if each movement would heal her
and this nightmare over.

The other family was so matter of fact. Their love
was action. What is the treatment?
When can it start? What is recommended?
They may have been afraid,
but they didn't show it.

I found the matter of fact mother in the day lounge
where parents went to take a break and regroup.
Tears coursing down her cheeks, heaving sobs
I put my hand out to her and she grasped it so tightly.
Saying over and over *oh I am so sorry* as if
she had no right to grieve, no right to cry.
After awhile I brought her a cup of tea
and clean tissues. She mopped her eyes, drank the tea
and went back to her child.

BECAUSE OF THE MOON

I sit up all night
walk outside to check out
the light splattered sky
glancing off the clouds

the big eye moon
slung up there
in charge of the sky and the night
winking at me challenging
Yeah Babe, try to sleep through this.

"Yes" he said he loved me then.
He "couldn't help it," he said, the beatings.
"Something took over," he said.
Yes, I said,
but your hands were brutal.

I thought of this then and my tears came
such deep tears.

With my neighborhood silent
on the wing, silent in place
a whisper through the trees
occasional wind gust. I walked
in the moonlight sat in the bole of a tree
listening.

The wind took me deep within my heart
and that mystery
spoke in a language
I somehow knew
and had longed for.

STOLEN PLANT

My friend, Sarah was showing me her plants. The ones she had
 replanted and that were doing well in their pots on the shelf in the
 sun in her kitchen.
"And this one," she pointed to a large white pot with a geranium in
 it, "was stolen from my front porch. I saw it on the neighbor's
 porch."
Sarah's house is not in the best part of town.
"I called the police," she continued. "Yes I did, I called them, they do a
 lot of drugs over there and I didn't want to just go over and ask for
 my plant back."
 So the police came and we went to the neighbor's house. The
 policeman knocked on the door and a woman came out. She
 looking all disheveled, has tobacco stains on her fingers and smells
 bad. He said to her, "Mam, where did you get this plant?" So the
 neighbor says, *well I don't know. It's mine, it's on my porch here.*
So the cop says, "Well Mam your neighbor here says it belongs to her,
 and she wants it back."
Oh is that so? says the neighbor looking antsy, *well I don't know
 nothing about that, Drunk Larry gave me that plant, you know
 Drunk Larry just up the street there a ways, but if it's yours you
 should take it.*
"Well it's mine," says my friend Sarah, and with that she picked up her
 plant and went home.

I GREET QUEEN ELIZABETH

Pushing my way to the front row I greet the Queen
I always seem to travel alone
Wanting to go where the moment takes me
An opening I can only take as one

I always seem to travel alone
Fearful to get off the boat in Hong Kong
An opening I can only take as one
The Universe gave me the help I needed

Fearful to get off the boat in Hong Kong
So far from home and quite alone
The Universe gave me the help I needed
Moving forward with the time

So far from home and quite alone
Wanting to go where the moment takes me
"Are you having a good Holiday?" I say to the Queen "Holiday!" she
    exclaims
Pushing my way to the front row I greet the Queen.

NIGHT RUN

Oh and into the pensive night
I ran then
with the leashed dogs.
And all at once letting go
feet sure and flying on the road
fast as ever I could.
The dogs racing with me
a huge sweep of energy
running in the dark,
the haven of dog walkers,
the haven of the night.

ABOUT THE AUTHOR

SUE SILVER is a poet and Practitioner of Energy Healing, Nurse Anesthetist and photographer. Born in New Zealand, she grew up there and in Australia, India, and the United States has lived in Tahiti, New Zealand, Australia and Hong Kong. She now lives in West Virginia. Her work has been published in *Lummox #3* (Lummox Press); *The Anthology of Appalachian Writers* Volumes III, IV and V; *Poetry and Prose; In Good Company; First Lights;* and www.danmurano.com: A journal of poetry and popular culture.

Sue has recorded her poetry for Grace Cavalieri's "The Poet and the Poem" series at the Library of Congress. She has read her work at Schaharazade, and Artomatic, (Jefferson County, WV;) and on WHSC, Shepherd University Radio, often co-hosting "Poetry Mondays" with John Case. Sue finds poetry to be a major vehicle for her work in Energy Medicine and Transformational Healing of the whole person.